Collins *Little book of*

Whisky

HarperCollins Publishers
Westerhill Road
Bishopbriggs
Glasgow
G64 2QT

First Edition 2014

Reprint 10 9 8 7 6 5 4 3

ISBN 978-0-00-752478-5

www.collins.co.uk

A catalogue record for this book is available from the British Library

Author: Dominic Roskrow

Typeset by
Davidson Publishing Solutions

Printed and bound in China at
RR Donnelley APS

Contents

Introduction

These are heady days for malt whisky in general, and Scotch whisky in particular.

For several years now, the demand for whisky worldwide has soared, benefiting from a combination of trends including a demand for products with established provenance and heritage, the move towards drinking less but better and towards quality over quantity, and the surge in demand for new and exciting cocktails.

Scotch whisky in particular has successfully positioned itself as an affordable luxury, an attainable status symbol, and a highly cherished gift in markets stretching from Russia to Mexico.

The boom for whisky has already stretched into years, and while there are plenty of people who warn of the dangers of bust to follow boom, and mutter darkly about previous crashes and the bursting of whisky bubbles, many others point to the number of emerging markets where Scotch Whisky is in its infancy, and the fact that there are scores of economies at different stages of their growth cycles, ensuring that the whisky industry has its eggs in several baskets and is insulated against a downturn in any one of them.

But while the surging demand for Scotch whisky is obviously great news for what is one of the United Kingdom's most lucrative industries, it doesn't come without its problems. Supply of spirit is under huge pressure, and whisky faces particular difficulty because of the lengthy time lags – at least three years and typically 10 or 12 years – before whisky can be produced and bottled in response to any new demand.

The result of this is an industry in a state of flux. It is responding to shortages in various ways, and there is a big schism between the two biggest whisky producers. On the one hand, drinks giant Diageo argues that the industry should put less emphasis on the importance of age to the quality of a good Scotch whisky and says that whisky should be judged entirely on how it tastes, irrespective of age. It points to the improvements in the quality of malt spirit due to better management of the wooden casks used in production.

On the other hand, French global producer Pernod Ricard, which is blessed with large stocks of very old whisky, is stressing age and its importance to the quality of great whisky, and commanding premium prices for the rarest and oldest malts.

What both sides agree on, however, is that demand for whisky cannot be met by single malt production alone. A distillery has a finite capacity, and it is impossible to increase it without a large investment in time and money. While both the big companies are building new distilleries, extending existing ones, and dusting down mothballed ones, they don't intend to wait 12–15 years for the spirit.

For this reason, the future of Scotch whisky lies in blended whisky. Blends are a mix of lots of malts and grain whisky, and the exact recipes are a closely guarded industry secret. That means that recipes can be tweaked and distillates added or dropped as required. In emerging markets, new consumers are being encouraged to move not from blended whisky to single malt whisky, but from blends to older or better blends.

Blended whisky still accounts for more than 90 per cent of whisky sales, and there are so many brands allocated to specific markets as to make documenting them all but impossible: to do so would require a book the size of the Bible. But blends are worth a mention because their burgeoning success is sucking malt whisky out of the market, and that affects what Scotland can offer in the single malt category.

This book sets out to cover the single malt distilleries currently operating in Scotland. Many of them produce whisky almost exclusively for the blended sector, and that has always been the case. Others are increasingly focusing on that sector. But that doesn't mean the end, or necessarily even the decline, of single malt whisky, because, ironically, the surge in global demand for blended whisky has opened the door to small independent malt producers.

The move towards brands such as Johnnie Walker, Chivas Regal and Ballantine's has left a shortfall in supply of single malt, and it is being filled by new distillers not just in Scotland but across the world, in countries as diverse as Australia, Sweden, Taiwan, Wales, India, France and South Africa. Barely a week goes by without a new distillery opening up, and of course we then have to wait at least three years to taste the products of their labour.

So this book is as up-to-date as it can be, and includes the more important distilleries yet to bottle spirit, and new ones that have yet to establish a core product.

It makes for a dynamic, exciting and evolving industry – not words you might always associate with Scotch.

So keep your eyes peeled – yet another new distillery might be just around the corner.

About the Author

Dominic Roskrow has written exclusively about whisky for 12 years, and about the drinks industry for more than 20. He edited *Whisky Magazine* for four years and currently writes for leading drinks titles *The Whisky Advocate* and *Drinks International*, as well as running his own business, The World Whisky Company. *Collins Little Book of Whisky: Malt Whiskies of Scotland* is the seventh book Dominic has written on whisky. As well as being a Keeper of The Quaich and a Kentucky Colonel, Dominic is also a passionate Leicester City and All Blacks fan.

Scotland's Whisky Regions

Scotland's malt whisky tends to be classified into the following broad regional and stylistic divisions:

Speyside: Home to about a third of Scotland's distilleries. The whiskies are complex, sophisticated and prized for their blending potential; the sweet end of the whisky spectrum.

Highlands: Full-bodied, rich and robust whiskies, with a complex array of flavours; often smoky and with an earthy, peaty quality.

Islands: A variety of styles, from clean and citrussy (Jura, Scapa) to bold and peated (Talisker, Highland Park).

Islay: Normally the most intense of whiskies: heavily peated and briny, with tar-like qualities. But Bunnahabhain and Bruichladdich demonstrate that the island has other styles too.

Lowlands: Light-bodied and usually light-hued, with grain, grassy and delicate floral notes.

Campbeltown: These whiskies are robust in character and carry the salty tang of the sea.

Whisky regions in Scotland

Scotland's malt distilleries by region

The distilleries are listed in alphabetical order on pages 14–122, while below we list them within the principal Scottish whisky regions.

Speyside
Aberlour
Allt-a-Bhainne
Auchroisk
Aultmore
Balmenach
Balvenie
BenRiach
Benrinnes
Benromach
Cardhu
Cragganmore
Craigellachie
Dailuaine
Dufftown
Glenallachie
Glenburgie
GlenDronach
Glendullan
Glen Elgin
Glenfarclas
Glenfiddich
Glen Grant
Glenlivet
Glenlossie
Glen Moray
Glenrothes
Glen Spey
Glentauchers
Inchgower
Kininvie
Knockando
Linkwood
Longmorn
Macallan
Macduff
Mannochmore
Miltonduff
Mortlach
Roseisle
Royal Brackla
Speyburn
Speyside
Strathisla
Strathmill
Tamdhu
Tamnavulin
Tomintoul
Tormore

Highlands
Aberfeldy
Ardmore
Balblair
Ben Nevis
Blair Athol
Clynelish
Dalmore
Dalwhinnie
Deanston
Edradour
Fettercairn
Glencadam
Glen Garioch
Glengoyne
Glenmorangie
Glen Ord
Glenturret
Knockdhu
Loch Lomond
Oban
Old Pulteney
Royal
 Lochnagar
Teaninich
Tomatin
Tullibardine

Islands
Abhainn Dearg
Arran
Highland Park
Jura
Scapa
Talisker
Tobermory

Islay
Ardbeg
Bowmore
Bruichladdich
Bunnahabhain
Caol Ila
Kilchoman
Lagavulin
Laphroaig
Port Charlotte

Lowlands
Ailsa Bay
Auchentoshan
Bladnoch
Daftmill
Glenkinchie

Campbeltown
Glengyle
Glen Scotia
Springbank

Aberfeldy

HIGHLANDS

Aberfeldy, Perthshire
www.aberfeldy.com
www.dewarsworldof
whisky.com

Core range
Aberfeldy 12-year-old
Aberfeldy 21-year-old

Signature malt
Aberfeldy 12-year-old:
rich, oily and fresh, with
a zesty tangerine note

A delightfully and beautifully maintained Highland distillery in a village close to Pitlochry, Aberfeldy is also home to Dewar's World of Whisky, an all-singing, all-dancing visitor centre celebrating the blended whisky to which Aberfeldy contributes. That tends to overshadow the malt which is made here a little, but it's starting to come into its own, with a series of single cask and retail-exclusive releases.

Aberlour

SPEYSIDE

Aberlour, Banffshire
www.aberlour.com

Core range
Aberlour 10-year-old
Aberlour 12- and 16-year-old
Double Cask Matured A'Bunadh

Signature malt
Aberlour 10-year-old:
surprisingly weighty and full, with honey and malt in balance and just a hint of the distillery's trademark mint notes

Nestled at the end of Aberlour's busy main street, Aberlour distillery remains largely as it was when completed in the 19th century. Tours here are among the best in Scotland, and the whiskies are diverse, fruity and satisfying. One of them, Aberlour A'Bunadh, is particularly noteworthy: it is made in batches, tends to be bottled around 60% abv, and is an industry pacesetter.

Abhainn Dearg

ISLANDS

Carnish, Isle of Lewis
www.abhainndearg.co.uk

This tiny craft distillery on the island of Lewis is one of Scotland's newest, and is the first legal distillery in The Outer Hebrides. Abhainn Dearg was only built in 2008 and so it has no core products or regular releases as yet. When it does, stocks are going to be very limited because the distillery is tiny, and output will be much less than many of its Scottish contemporaries.

There is no precedent for the style of whisky from this part of the world but perhaps unsurprisingly the distillery has opted for a peaty style, partly because it is fashionable and in demand, and probably because it's easier to market young, peated whisky at an early age. Indeed, in 2011 it produced rough and ready peated whisky at three years old – the legal minimum – and in 2013 bottled a five year old version.

It'll be a while yet before the whisky's true characteristics become known, but as there are few trees on Lewis and so little tree root in the vegetation that forms the peat, it's likely to have much in common with the sweet smoky flavours of Islay.

Ailsa Bay

LOWLANDS

Grangestone Industrial Estate, Ayrshire
www.williamgrant.com

When is a Lowland distillery not a Lowland distillery? When it's Ailsa Bay. And if the address hardly conjures up images of rolling bens, pretty glens and bubbling lochs, that's because this distillery means business. It is owned by William Grant & Sons and has been built on the site of the family's huge grain plant in Ayr, which it built to protect it from market vagaries and the business practices of its rivals.

It's an oddball distillery in several ways. It exists pretty much exclusively to provide more malt for the company's extensive blending business, which is prospering worldwide. It's also an experimental distillery, used by the company to try new flavours and whisky styles; something they have proved adept at in the past. And the style of whisky has more in common with its sisters Glenfiddich and Balvenie in Speyside than it does with The Lowlands.

However, its geography says it is a Lowland distillery, and the region – once rich in big production distilleries – needs all the help it can get.

Allt-a-Bhainne

SPEYSIDE

Glenrinnes, Dufftown, Banffshire
www.pernodricard.com
www.chivas.com

Seagrams built Allt-a-Bhainne along with Braeval Distillery in the 1970s. The construction was to help meet the growing demand for blended whisky, and Allt-a-Bhainne has only ever been a provider of malt for blends. Consequently, its fate has been tied to that of blended whiskies per se. It was mothballed in 2002 but reopened three years later when current owner Pernod Ricard needed more malt to expand output of its newly acquired Chivas Regal brand.

Allt-a-Bhainne is a large distillery, producing an estimated four million litres of spirit each year, and is designed to operate with the minimum number of people. There are no official malt bottlings, but some malt is occasionally bottled independently.

Ardbeg

ISLAY

Port Ellen, Isle of Islay
www.ardbeg.com

Core range
Ardbeg 10-year-old
Corryvreckan
Uigedail
Alligator

Signature malt
Ardbeg 10-year-old: a meal in a glass; cocoa, oily fish, swirling peat and chewy sweetness married together perfectly; truly exceptional

South Islay's whiskies are famous for their distinctive peaty, smoky style, and Ardbeg is one of the "big three" distilleries that sit next to each other in what might be called whisky nirvana. The sea laps across the rocky shoreline right up to the distillery walls, and arguably there are few experiences finer than drinking malt here, straight from the cask on a blustery and sunny Islay day. If peaty, tangy, tarry and oily whisky is your thing, you will find Ardbeg to be sublime.

In addition to the core range, cask strength bottlings and a few oddballs are also on offer. Very Young, Still Young, Almost There and Renaissance track the maturation of the signature 10-year-old from six years up to full maturity. There are also some fantastic special bottlings originally casked before 1980. Be warned though: Ardbeg can easily become a very expensive lifelong pursuit.

The word "quaint" might have been invented for Ardbeg, and a ramshackle tour here takes you past hand-painted signs and a medley of traditional distilling equipment. It ends in what used to be the kiln for malting barley and is now one of the finest cafés in Scotland.

Ardmore

HIGHLANDS

Kennethmont,
Aberdeenshire

Signature malt
Ardmore Traditional Cask: lightly peated, non-chill filtered and bottled at 46% abv to maximise the natural flavours

Ardmore annually produces about five million litres of malt. It is mainly destined for the Teacher's blend, but an increasing amount is released as a single malt. As at sister distillery Laphroaig, some of Ardmore's whisky is matured in quarter-sized casks to develop the malt flavour further.

As for the whisky, Ardmore Traditional Cask is a peated malt that enjoys the highest quality maturation – first in ex-bourbon barrels and then in traditional quarter casks.

Arran

ISLANDS

Lochranza, Isle of Arran
www.arranwhisky.com

Core range
Arran 10-year-old
The Arran Malt
Arran 100 proof
Robert Burns Single Malt
Cask bottlings

Signature malt
Arran 10-year-old:
creamy, rich mix of
citrus, toffee and
butterscotch; very chewy
and quite delightful

Arran has something of a scattergun approach to releasing malts, and in the early days released some ropey young whiskies. But by the time the distillery was bottling a 10-year-old it had turned into a glorious swan of a malt. Its rich creaminess is credited to its location at Lochranza, where it sits in a suntrap in the Gulf Stream. Recent cask strength and non chill-filtered versions of the malt are particularly impressive. Also keep an eye out for one of the occasional special cask finishes.

Auchentoshan

LOWLANDS

Clydebank, Glasgow
www.auchentoshan.com

Core range
Auchentoshan Select,
Auchentoshan 12-, 18- and 21-year-olds
Auchentoshan Three Wood

Signature malt
Auchentoshan 12-year-old: light and smooth, with a hint of citrus; very accessible to the beginner

Auchentoshan is special because it is a triple distilled single malt. It bears the trademark characteristics of a Lowland malt in that it is light and easy to drink. But some of the more recent bottlings show a surprising and impressive diversity. It's worth comparing the clean, subtle and citrussy 18-year-old alongside the Three Wood, for example – the latter drenched in sherry flavours. The Limited Editions are fantastic examples of the very best Auchentoshan casks.

Auchroisk

SPEYSIDE

Ulben, Banffshire
www.malts.com

Signature malt
Auchroisk 10-year-old

Special occasions
Auchroisk 28-year-old Rare Malt

Producing 3.1 million litres each year, Auchroisk is a relatively modern distillery, built in 1974 to supply what was then the International Distiller and Vintner group (IDV) with malt for blending.

The choice of location was taken after careful consideration and so, perhaps unsurprisingly, the distillery's malt proved to be of high quality. Some of it has been bottled as a single malt since the mid-1980s. Early bottlings were known as The Singleton, but the distillery's name is now used.

Aultmore

SPEYSIDE

Keith, Banffshire

Signature malt
Aultmore 12-year-old

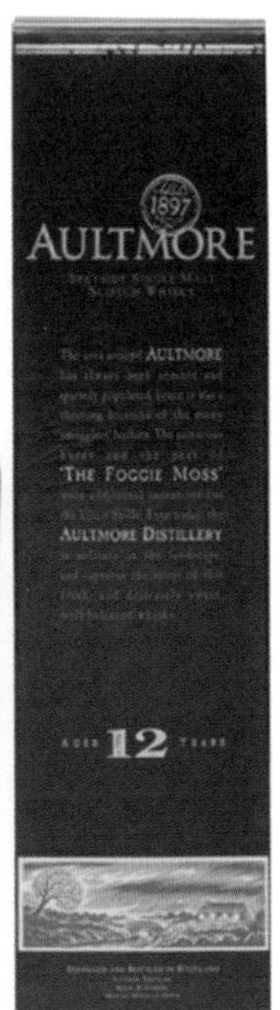

Only a tiny fraction of the whisky produced at Aultmore is bottled as a single malt, with the vast majority being used for blending purposes. Unsurprisingly, then, this is a clean, consistent, no-nonsense malt. The distillery started producing in 1897 and has been in demand pretty much ever since.

There may not be much Aultmore around as single malt, but if you are interested in exploring this whisky further, it would be worth seeking out some independent bottlings, such as those produced by Elgin-based bottlers Gordon & MacPhail.

Balblair

HIGHLANDS

Edderton, Ross-Shire
www.balblair.com

Core range
Vintage 2001
Vintage 1989
Vintage 1979

Signature malt
Vintage 2001: Balblair is known for its full-bodied, clean, rich and fruity whiskies, and while this isn't over-complicated, it's a classic in the distillery style.

Balblair has worked to reposition the distillery's malts to focus on vintage bottlings rather than the standard age expressions. That, along with impressive premium packaging, suggests Balblair is a malt that's going places. They say that the air around the distillery is the purest in Scotland, and Balblair associates itself with this purity. But Balblair isn't a lightweight, and has some distinctive earthy and spicy flavours that make it an attractive and satisfying malt.

Balmenach

SPEYSIDE

Cromdale, Grantown-on-Spey

Balmenach produces whisky almost exclusively for blending, so bottlings as single malts are extremely rare. A 12-year-old has appeared in the past, though, and some of the distillery's sizeable output finds its way into independent bottling.

Balvenie

SPEYSIDE

Dufftown, Banffshire
www.thebalvenie.com

Core range
DoubleWood 12-year-old
DoubleWood 17-year-old
14-year-old Rum Cask
Single Barrel 15-year-old
PortWood 21-year-old
30-year-old

Signature malt
DoubleWood 12-year-old: chewy rich fruits and the most exquisite Speyside honey

Special occasions
The 21-year-old is quite possibly the best example there is of a whisky finished in port pipes, but the 30-year-old is a world-class big hitter, dressed in ermine

Balvenie is the sister distillery to Glenfiddich, the world's biggest malt distillery. What it lacks in scale and quantity, Balvenie more than makes up for in quality, with its fruity, honeyed whiskies.

Balvenie is situated on the same site as Glenfiddich and owner William Grant's third distillery, Kininvie. Balvenie's output is very much as a whisky lover's whisky, its distinctive toffeeness earning it a reputation as one of Speyside's top whiskies. It is the perfect foil to the glitzy Glenfiddich: a traditional craft distillery that does things the old-fashioned way.

Balvenie has been earning a reputation for fine malt through a series of vintage releases, and its VIP is as good as any in the world. Leave four hours for an in-depth tour, conducted in all likelihood by someone with 40-50 years' distillery experience, and a sublime and extensive tasting at the end.

Ben Nevis

HIGHLANDS

Lochy Bridge, Fort William
www.bennevisdistillery.com

Signature malt
Ben Nevis 10-year-old

Special occasions
Ben Nevis 13-year-old
Port Finish

The stunning location and a sympathetic refurbishment by its Japanese owners draw visitors to Ben Nevis. The distillery has had a chequered past, but is now approaching its 20th anniversary since the acquisition by Japan's second-largest distiller, Nikka, and a steady flow of quality 10-year-old and the occasional special bottling have established it as a solid malt producer. Ben Nevis is one of the very few distilleries that bottles a single malt and a blend under the same name, so check what you're buying. The distillery also sells its own Glencoe blend, which is eight years old.

BenRiach

SPEYSIDE

Longmorn, near Elgin, Morayshire
www.benriachdistillery.co.uk

Core range
Curiositas 10-year-old
Heart of Speyside
12-year-old
15-year-old
Birnie Moss
20-year-old
30-year-old

Signature malt
BenRiach 12-year-old: with a classic and superb Speyside character – all rich fruit and honey, held in place by a balanced oak and malt lining

The team behind this distillery now has two others, and it has hardly put a foot wrong in the last decade. The highly talented Billy Walker has put out all sorts of oddball whiskies under the BenRiach moniker, but they are rarely anything but excellent. Rum cask finishes are particularly impressive. Oddly for Speyside, some of the whiskies are peated, but if that's your bag and you're feeling flush, the 21-year-old Authenticus is a world classic.

Benrinnes

SPEYSIDE

Aberlour, Banffshire
www.malts.com

Signature malt
Benrinnes 15-year-old

This is another of Diageo's production distilleries, producing malt for a range of blends, and with little whisky released as single malt. It produces a healthy 2.6 million litres of spirit each year.

There are technical points of interest at Benrinnes. It is one of just a handful of distilleries using the "worm tub" method to condense the spirit. The method is so named because of the worm-like horizontal pipes which lie in a tank of cool, flowing water.

The other unusual feature is that its six stills are arranged in two groups of three, with one wash still feeding two spirits stills.

Benromach

SPEYSIDE

Forres, Moray
www.benromach.com

Core range
Benromach Traditional, Organic
 and Peat Smoke
Tokaji
Sassicaia
Portwood
Benromach 25-year-old

Signature malt
Benromach Traditional: a delicate mix of malt and fruit with a spicy afterglow and a trace of smoke

Special occasions
Benromach 21-year-old: a heady mix of sherry, dark fruits, oak and spice - exquisite

Owner Gordon & MacPhail is a leading exponent of good wood management, and when it bought this cute distillery it set about trying all sorts of unusual things. So, despite its tiny size, it's one of the most varied and experimental distilleries in Scotland. It is well worth a visit should you be anywhere close.

Bladnoch

LOWLANDS

Wigtown, Wigtownshire
www.bladnoch.co.uk

Core range
Bladnoch 10-, 12-, 13- and 15-year-olds

Signature malt
Bladnoch 10-year-old: almost defines the Lowland style, with floral and light citrus notes and a complex mix of other influences

Special occasions
Bladnoch 15-year-old: the cask strength is chewier, more intense and deeper than the normal bottlings

Bladnoch is a very small, isolated and pretty distillery, and produces a style of whisky that for a long time was deeply neglected – the light, floral, Lowland type. Despite its size, Bladnoch offers tours and tastings. About 25,000 visitors make their way to the distillery each year, and few of them leave disappointed.

Blair Athol

HIGHLANDS

Pitlochry, Perthshire
www.discovering-distilleries.com

Signature malt
Blair Athol 12-year-old:
unfussy and richly fruity

Special occasions
A very rare 27-year-old is worth investigation – if you can find a bottle

Blair Athol lies close to the A9, not far from Edradour Distillery, in the region of the Highlands to the south of Speyside. It is a sizeable distillery, capable of producing about two million litres a year. But very little of this is bottled as a single malt, and it has just one core expression, the Blair Athol 12-year-old. The vast majority of its malt output goes into the heart of Bell's blended whisky.

The distillery is one of the oldest working distilleries in Scotland, having been established in 1798, a century before many others close to it.

Bowmore

ISLAY

Bowmore, Isle of Islay
www.bowmore.com

Core range
Bowmore 12-, 15-, 18- and 25-year-olds

Signature malt
Bowmore 12-year-old: the classic Bowmore, with a lovely balance of oak, malt, sea notes and mid-range peat smoke

Special occasions
Bowmore 18-year-old: this is a delight. The balance of floating smoke, fruit and oak wrap around the distinctive and chunky malt perfectly

The town of Bowmore lies halfway across the island, and its whiskies are among Scotland's most famous. A few years back the distillery was floundering a little, but since 2012 it has been on a roll, with some fabulous big peaty whiskies, such as various beauties under the Tempest moniker, which rival the island's very best. There are some great but expensive old expressions too.

Bowmore is a wonderful place to visit too. It improved its facilities a couple of years ago and now has a visitor centre that boasts stunning views across Loch Indaal to Bruichladdich Distillery. When the breeze is up and the sun flits across the busy waves that lap up to the distillery, take a glass of Bowmore and drink it whilst sitting on the sea wall – you'll never feel more alive!

Bowmore also has its own floor maltings and huge peat-burning fires, so you can see and smell the work in progress.

Bruichladdich

ISLAY

Bruichladdich, Isle of Islay
www.bruichladdich.com

Core range
Bruichladdich 10-, 12- and 15-year-olds
Bruichladdich XVII

Signature malt
Bruichladdich 10-year-old: clean, unpeaty, sweet and fruity; very moreish

Special occasions
Bruichladdich XVII: very fresh – almost zesty – and on its best behaviour, but with enough bite for interest

Bruichladdich was – and maybe still is – something of a whisky anorak's darling, having been reopened in 2000 by a dedicated and popular team and run independently. With the highly respected whisky legend Jim McEwan at the helm, for a decade or so it was some ride. It has always been a bit of a maverick, has released scores of expressions of varying quality, and demonstrated an admirable irreverence while never missing a marketing opportunity. It built a reputation as the people's distillery, throwing its doors open to visitors and never missing the chance to niggle the big producers. But it's evolving fast: in the summer of 2012 the management team announced that it was selling it at a top-end price to French giant Remy Cointreau. And with stock aged more than 12 years produced since the reopening, there's an opportunity for focus and development. Whisky fans are watching with interest.

Bunnahabhain

ISLAY

Port Askaig, Isle of Islay
www.bunnahabhain.com

Core range
Bunnahabhain 12-, 18- and 25-year-olds

Signature malt
Bunnahabhain 12-year-old

Special occasions
Bunnahabhain 25-year-old: a weighty whisky, with rich plum and sherry notes

Pronounced "Boon-a-hah-ven", this was known as the gentle malt of Islay, but a few years back the strength of the malt was raised, the "chill filtering" method of removing fats and flavour congeners was stopped so more flavour was left in, and this whisky grew up. Peated versions are also available. A whisky to re-explore if you fell out with it years ago.

Caol Ila

ISLAY

Port Askaig, Islay
www.malts.com

Core range
Caol Ila 12-, 18- and 25-year-olds
Caol Ila Cask Strength

Signature malt
Caol Ila 12-year-old: oily, with a seaside barbecue combination of smoky bacon and grilled sardines

Caol Ila is the biggest whisky producer on Islay. It's not the best known, however, as most of its malt goes into blends, particularly Johnnie Walker. In 2001 – and partly because of stock problems at owner Diageo's other peated Islay whisky Lagavulin – Caol Ila started to be sold as a single malt in three expressions. It has since become the island's fastest growing malt – which is no wonder, as this is a truly special whisky, and the 18-year-old, in particular, is up there with the very best.

Cardhu

SPEYSIDE

Aberlour, Banffshire
www.malts.com

Signature malt
Cardhu 12-year-old: sweet, very malty, very clean and very drinkable

Cardhu is the symbolic home of Johnnie Walker, and its malt is a main component in the range of Walker blends. But, for all its high-profile associations, Cardhu exists in a whisky limbo-land. It enjoys a huge market in Southern Europe, particularly in Spain, and is much in demand for blending. In certain circles, it is even regarded as malt at its very finest. Yet it receives none of the acclaim in its homeland that's usually reserved for great Speysiders; it attracts a relatively small number of visitors too. More's the pity, as it is a charming distillery.

Clynelish

HIGHLANDS

Brora, Sutherland
www.malts.com

Signature malt
Clynelish 14-year-old

Clynelish is rather enigmatic. It has the characteristics of both a seaside malt and a Highland one. Furthermore, it is situated in the town of Brora, next to another distillery that was originally called Clynelish but changed its name to Brora. For a short time, the two distilleries operated side by side as Clynelish 1 and 2, before the older one closed.

Clynelish now produces a rich and smoky malt, and is highly recommended. But it's nowhere near as peaty as the original Clynelish style and the other whiskies produced at Brora.

Cragganmore

SPEYSIDE

Ballindalloch, Banffshire
www.discovering-distilleries.com

Signature malt
Cragganmore 12-year-old: complex and rich Speyside fruit with a much less typically Speyside tangy undertow

Special occasions
Cragganmore 17-year-old: bottled at cask strength and limited to a few thousand bottles

Cragganmore, one of the smallest distilleries owned by drinks corporation Diageo, is a sophisticated sweet-and-sour fruit mix of a whisky. It is one of Diageo's six "classic malts", representing the Speyside region in that collection, though it is not entirely typical of Speyside in its character.

Craigellachie

SPEYSIDE

Craigellachie, Aberlour

Signature malt
Craigellachie 14-year-old: a nice mix of malt spice and fruit. Unchallenging but perfectly palatable

The village of Craigellachie is situated in the very heart of Speyside, alongside the rivers Spey and Fiddich. For many years the main hotel in the village has been seen as a base camp for all good whisky expeditions. The Craigellachie distillery itself is not very exciting, though – its featureless glass front and garish red lettering are suggestive of a factory rather than a malt producer. Very little Craigellachie is bottled as single malt, most being used by Dewar & Sons.

Daftmill

LOWLANDS

By Cupar, Fife
www.daftmilldistillery.com

Along with Glengyle in Campbeltown, Daftmill is a highly unusual new distillery, in that while most distilleries are under immense pressure to produce a whisky as soon as it's legal to do so at three years old, Daftmill has yet to bottle anything after nine years. It's a luxury few can afford, and many have come unstuck producing whisky that is too young.

However, the wait is nearly over – next year, brothers Ian and Francis Cuthbert, who have continued their business as farmers while making whisky as an aside, will finally bottle a fully formed and no doubt delightful tasting 10-year-old Lowland malt. Because of the lighter style of Lowland whisky, this should be an ample age for the spirit.

Daftmill is one of a growing number of craft distilleries shooting up in Scotland, ensuring an independent Scotch whisky market at least for the foreseeable future.

Dailuaine

SPEYSIDE

Aberlour, Banffshire
www.malts.com

Signature malt
Dailuaine 16-year-old

Founded in 1852, Dailuaine has been in almost continuous production for 155 years, except for three years between 1917 and 1920, when it was closed due to fire damage. With the potential to produce more than three million litres of spirit a year, Dailuaine is one of Scotland's biggest malt contributors, yet one of its least known. That is because only a small percentage of the spirit made here makes it into single malt bottlings; most is used for Johnnie Walker blends, such as the classic Black Label.

Dalmore

HIGHLANDS

Alness, Ross-shire
www.thedalmore.com

Core range
The Dalmore 12
The Dalmore 15
The Dalmore 18
1263 King Alexander III

Signature malt
The Dalmore 12-year-old: muscular, with orange notes and a solid oak and malt platform

Special occasions
The Dalmore 1263 King Alexander III: stunning and complex mix of bourbon notes, sherry and rich fruit

Dalmore breaks records at its most premium end, and has been stylishly repackaged and reshaped at the entry level. This is a big, tasty and impressive example of Highland malt at its best.

Dalwhinnie

HIGHLANDS

Dalwhinnie, Inverness-shire
www.malts.com

Signature malt
Dalwhinnie 15-year-old: whisky's answer to a Harlan Coben crime novel, twisting its way into and out of taste cul-de-sacs at breathtaking pace, before reaching an unexpected but totally satisfying climax. Earthy, smoky, swampy, overwhelming – a thoroughly recommended whisky

Dalwhinnie is in the heart of the Highlands, and at a little over 1000 feet above sea level is one of Scotland's highest distilleries. But it's just off the A9 and easy to find, and it produces one of the region's very best malts, a great combination of rugged peatiness and sweet honey.

Deanston

HIGHLANDS

Deanston, nr Doune, Perthshire

Signature malt
Deanston 12-year-old: reliable rather than flashy, with clean honey and malt notes

Special occasions
Deanston 30-year-old Single Malt Limited Edition: a veritable old gent - the years in cask have given it great depth, with a tangy, spicy edge

Deanston is a lovely distillery to visit, its workings neatly slotted into an old cotton mill and with a stylish new visitor centre and tour. The malt itself has been revamped and at 12 years old is now much more assertive and enjoyable. The site boasts its own hydro-electric power station.

Dufftown

SPEYSIDE

Dufftown, Keith, Banffshire
www.malts.com

Signature malt
Flora & Fauna 15-year-old

Special occasions
The Singleton of Dufftown

A sizeable Diageo distillery making malt primarily for blends, and in particular Bell's. It is made from a distillery beer fermented for a particularly long time, perhaps explaining its fruitiness. But perhaps its biggest claim to fame is as the malt used in the United Kingdom version of whisky called The Singleton.

Edradour

HIGHLANDS

Pitlochry, Perthshire
www.edradour.co.uk

Signature malt
Edradour 10-year-old

Special occasions
Edradour 30-year-old

Edradour is independently owned by the bottler Signatory, which is headed up by Andrew Symington. The distillery has launched a host of unusual whiskies, many of which are bottled straight from the cask, and it is also experimenting with peat levels and unusual finishes. The popularity of Edradour as a visitor attraction is remarkable, given that it is one of Scotland's smallest distilleries. It makes just 12 casks of whisky a week, and getting hold of the drink is not always easy. But Edradour commands huge loyalty from those who have discovered it, particularly if they have visited the distillery.

Fettercairn

HIGHLANDS

Laurencekirk, Kincardineshire
www.whyteandmackay.co.uk

Signature malt
Fettercairn Fior

Fettercairn was licensed in 1824, making it one of the oldest legal distilleries in Scotland. But it has had a mixed history, and to this day has been something of a misfit. The distillery itself is a pleasing one, set in the most rustic of environments and close to the pretty Georgian village of the same name.

Fettercairn has been repackaged in recent years but has struggled to assert itself. A real pity, because at very old ages it can be quite extraordinary.

Glenallachie

SPEYSIDE

Aberlour, Banffshire

Glenallachie was founded in 1967 and has been a sizeable contributor to a range of blended whiskies ever since. It was the last distillery to be designed by the great distillery architect of the 20th century, William Delmé-Evans, who died in 2002.

It's a modern and functional distillery which uses water taken from a spring on nearby Ben Rinnes. The malt is mainly used in blends and its current lifeline was established in 1989 when it was taken over by Pernod Ricard. Single bottlings are rare. A cask strength version aged about 15 years was released in 2005.

The whisky itself is delicate and floral, a pleasant Speysider worth seeking out if you can.

Glenburgie

SPEYSIDE

Forres, Morayshire

Glenburgie is a tale of two eras. The original distillery, dating from 1829, hit top gear in the late 1950s, when it was expanded to help meet the demand for malts to put into blended whisky. It housed two Lomond stills – tall pot stills with plates in the neck designed to alter the reflux of the still. However, the Lomond stills were very hard to maintain, and ceased to be used. Malt produced at this time occasionally appears under the name Glencraig.

The modern era began in 2005, after the distillery had been rebuilt at a cost of more than £4 million. Bottlings are very rare but worth seeking out. The whisky has gingery and dark chocolate characteristics, offering an unusual and pleasing experience.

Glencadam

HIGHLANDS

Brechin, Angus
www.angusdundee.co.uk

Signature malt
Glencadam 15-year-old

When it closed in 2000, Glencadam looked like it had gone for good, but just three years later it was bought by Angus Dundee Distillers and brought back to life.

As under its previous ownership, most of Glencadam's whisky is destined for a range of blends, including Ballantine's, Teacher's and Stewart's Cream of the Barley.

However, Glencadam is something of a hidden gem, and the release of a 15-year-old from the distillery was welcomed in a number of quarters. That's not at all surprising, because it's an extremely drinkable and pleasant malt.

GlenDronach

SPEYSIDE

Forgue, near Huntly

Signature malt
GlenDronach 15-year-old Revival: a deliberate return to the old days of big, spent match and stewed red fruits sherried malt.

Special occasions
Glendronach 33-year-old: sherry cask perfection, with toffee, Crunchie bar and a mouth-watering wood and malt balance; stands up to its age

GlenDronach has a surprisingly large, loyal following, but it lost its way a few years back and it took the intervention of the team behind BenRiach to put it back on track. It was known for big, sherried old-style malt. A traditional whisky from a traditional distillery – and thriving after coming back from the brink.

Glendullan

SPEYSIDE

Dufftown, Keith, Banffshire
www.malts.com

Special occasions
All the Glendullan Rare Malts are worth tasting, but they can be hard to find

The Glendullan Distillery can produce 3.7 million litres a year, yet it is virtually unknown as a single malt whisky in the UK. In the US, though, Diageo has bottled the whisky under its umbrella name "The Singleton", and it is being warmly received.

In the UK, a 12-year-old Glendullan was available for a while, and some is sold as an 8-year-old through supermarkets. Glendullan was chosen as the Speaker's whisky by Betty Boothroyd, Speaker of the House of Commons, in 1992, and there was a special bottling to celebrate the distillery's centenary in 1997.

Glen Elgin

SPEYSIDE

Longmorn, Elgin, Morayshire
www.malts.com

Signature malt
Glen Elgin 12-year-old

Special occasions
Glen Elgin 32-year-old

Few distilleries have had a more rocky existence and survived to tell the tale. Opened at the beginning of the 20th century, just as the industry was falling in on itself, Glen Elgin was closed and sold four times in its first six years. Today, it is owned by the drinks giant Diageo.

Glen Elgin attracts attention from enthusiasts because it has six worm tubs for condensing the spirit – a slow method that produces a characterful whisky. Besides a few special bottlings that have been released, Glen Elgin is most closely associated with the White Horse blend.

Glenfarclas

SPEYSIDE

Ballindalloch, Banffshire
www.glenfarclas.co.uk

Core range
Glenfarclas 10-, 12-, 15-, 17-, 21-, 25-, 30-, 40- and 50-year-olds
Glenfarclas 105 Cask Strength

Signature malt
Glenfarclas 12-year-old: more fruit and oak than the 10-year-old, and lashings of sweet malt

Special occasions
Glenfarclas 30-year-old: rich, fruit cake chewiness and lots of chocolate and orange – wonderful

Despite the competitive demands of a global market, there is still something wonderfully old-fashioned about Glenfarclas. It eschews any form of gimmickry, focusing instead on its strengths – malts produced in top-quality sherry casks. These are robust whiskies that stand up well to ageing – hence the 40- and 50-year-old expressions.

Glenfiddich

SPEYSIDE

Dufftown, Banffshire
www.glenfiddich.com

Core range
Special Reserve 12-year-old
Caoran Reserve 12-year-old
Solera Reserve 15-year-old
Ancient Reserve 18-year-old
Glenfiddich 30-year-old

Signature malt
Special Reserve 12-year-old: no frills fruity Speysider with the drinkability factor turned up high

Special occasions
The rich, soft and lush chocolate flavours in the 30-year-old are worth seeking out

Glenfiddich is the single malt that lit the touch paper to start the malt whisky explosion. It began in the 1960s and, in the UK at least, "Glenfiddich" soon became synonymous with "malt whisky".

Glenfiddich's owner, William Grant, was not only the first company to promote a single malt, but was also the first to open up the secrets of the malt world by opening a visitor centre. No fan of malt whisky should ever forget that, and nor should this whisky be dismissed as a novice's whisky just because it has been around so long. It has maintained its position as the world's biggest selling malt for good reason.

Glenfiddich's owner has continued to invest in the distillery to make sure that it still has a home worthy of its world status, and everything here is stylish and impressive. And because Glenfiddich shares a site with the traditional and more "serious" malt distillery Balvenie, there is something here for both beginner and seasoned whisky enthusiast.

Experts agree that it's producing its finest malt at the moment, and there have been several excellent limited edition releases.

Glen Garioch

HIGHLANDS

Meldrum, Aberdeenshire
www.glengarioch.com

Core range
Glen Garioch 12-year-old
Glen Garioch 15-year-old
Glen Garioch Founder's Reserve
Various vintages

Signature malt
Glen Garioch 15-year-old: an excellent introduction to Highland malt – a touch of oak and smoke around a mass of malt, and with green fruit and a distinctive Glen Garioch earthiness

The distillery is a step back in time and well worth a visit. The whisky is hard to categorize, but the diversity of expressions never stray from the fact that this is truly wonderful whisky. Very much a hidden but emerging gem.

Glengoyne

HIGHLANDS

Drumgoyne, near Killearn
www.glengoyne.com

Core range
Glengoyne 10-, 12-, 17-, 21- and 28-year-olds

Signature malt
Glengoyne 10-year-old: clean, crisp fruity malt that shows off all the distillery characteristics

Special occasions
The 16-year-old Scottish Oak, if you can get it, or the 21-year-old, which has a creamy quality and some deep, fruity, almost blood orange, notes

Glengoyne's pretty, 200-year-old distillery is set in a wooded area associated with Rob Roy, and it is one of the few surviving distilleries in this part of Scotland. Unchallenging, clean and pure tasting, Glengoyne whiskies are easy to drink and ideal for the novice. However, an extensive range of older and vintage malts guarantees a challenge for the more experienced palate, too.

Glen Grant

SPEYSIDE

Rothes, Morayshire

Core range
Glen Grant (no age)
Glen Grant 5-year-old
Glen Grant 10-year-old

Signature malt
Glen Grant: clean and crisp, like a green apple

Special occasions
Gordon & MacPhail have some Glen Grant that's been aged for more than 30 years – well worth exploring!

Glen Grant sits in the heart of Speyside but has a personality and charm like no other in the region. The whisky itself is pale and young. Bottles of Glen Grant are sold by the millions in mainland Europe, particularly in Italy, but surprisingly little elsewhere. The Italian drinks giant Campari bought it in 2006.

Glengyle

CAMPBELTOWN

Springbank, Campbeltown
www.kilkerran.com

Until a few years ago, the whisky industry around Campbeltown – once the beating heart of the Scotch whisky export business – was on its last legs and in danger of disappearing altogether, but thanks to the Mitchell family, it has turned a significant corner. One can only imagine the pride they must have felt in this part of the world when Campbeltown was given an official regional status.

The former site of the closed Glengyle distillery was bought by the owners of nearby Springbank, and spirit production began in 2004. The name Glengyle is registered, so the whisky the new distillery is making is called Kilkerran, and so far no official bottlings have been released, although there has been a small batch of 'works in progress'. The whisky has pleasant peatiness but with lots of sweetness, and spirit is being matured in rum and port casks as well as sherry and bourbon. One to watch out for.

Glenkinchie

LOWLANDS

Pencaitland, Tranent, East Lothian
www.discovering-distilleries.com

Core range
Glenkinchie 12-year-old
Distillers' Edition 14-year-old

Signature malt
Glenkinchie 12-year-old: light and easy with a hint of ginger

With Edinburgh just a bus ride away, Glenkinchie is the nearest thing the Scottish capital has to its own malt, and it would be all too easy to dismiss this as a token malt – light, refined and suitably easy on the palate to reflect the more genteel face of Scotland. It is, however, a quality whisky, with a dry, spicy finish.

Glenkinchie represents the Lowlands in Diageo's original Classic Malts range. Its gentle personality makes it an ideal aperitif whisky.

Glenlivet

SPEYSIDE

Ballindalloch, Banffshire
www.theglenlivet.com

Core range
The Glenlivet 12-, 15-,
18 and 21-year-olds
The Glenlivet XXV
Nadurra
1972 Cask Strength

Signature malt
The Glenlivet 18-year-old: not only a signature malt but also classic Speyside, with rich apple and berry fruits, and clean, fresh malt

Special occasions
The French Oak Reserve is wonderful, but if you're at a duty-free shop stocking the Nadurra 16-year-old, that's the one. Look for the cask strength version, with lashings of malt, chocolate and spice

The first licensed distillery in Scotland is also one of its best. As a place to visit, as a producer of exceptional whisky and in historical terms too, Glenlivet has very few rivals on Speyside. The distillery's owner, Pernod Ricard, wants Glenlivet malt to challenge Glenfiddich for the number one spot worldwide, and the distillery is growing its core brands with this in mind. However, the company also has to satisfy the thirst of enthusiasts for rarer malts from the archives, making the distillery both commercial and esoteric. Glenlivet has even let its whisky veteran Jim Cryle have his own mini-still, so that twice a year he can distil spirit in the way that it would have been 200 years ago.

What a great combination: a distillery with superb whisky; a couple of enthusiastic eccentrics at the helm; and enough tales of derring-do in the distillery's history to fill a *Boy's Own* annual several times over.

Glenlossie

SPEYSIDE

Elgin, Morayshire
www.malts.com

Signature malt
Flora & Fauna 10-year-old

Glenlossie sits next door to another distillery, Mannochmore, and shares the same workforce and warehouses. The distilleries are chalk and cheese, with Mannochmore built in the 1970s and Glenlossie established a whole century earlier. These days Glenlossie is part of the Diageo empire and is used mainly for blending, where it enjoys a strong reputation. It operates only between October and March, though its output is highly rated by whisky blenders.

Glenlossie is a rarity as a single malt but is highly regarded for its outstanding quality, so look out for any independent bottling. A limited edition 10-year-old was released in the early 90s as part of the Flora and Fauna series.

Glenmorangie

HIGHLANDS

Tain, Ross-shire
www.glenmorangie.com

Core range
Glenmorangie Original
Nectar D'or
Lasanta
Quinta Ruban

Signature malt
Glenmorangie Original: complex spice and oak dance around the malt with gay abandon and thrilling effect

Special occasions
In recent years Glenmorangie has bottled some wonderful and varied malts such as Ealanta, and they're all worth trying. For a splash of luxury, though, it has to be Signet.

Glenmorangie may be one of the giants of whisky, and therefore taken for granted by some, but it is also among a handful that spare no expense in sourcing the finest oak in which to mature their whisky. The quality of the malt here is going from strength to strength and, to highlight that fact, the distillery overhauled its range in late 2007.

The Nectar d'Or spends 10 years in ex-bourbon casks, followed by a spell in ex-Sauternes wine barriques. It is heavy on the flavour, but the lemon, grapefruit and spice are attractive enough. The Lasanta is a new look; new taste, but fine Glenmorangie with sherry wrapping and an enjoyable nuttiness. Quinta Ruban is matured in ex-bourbon casks, then finished in port pipes from wine estates – called quintas – in Portugal.

Some distilleries just drip with style and class, and this is one of them. If you're wanting to really spoil yourself, stay in a country house nearby and live like a laird for a while. When you explore the estate, first visit the Tarlogie spring that releases its precious mineral-rich water after a few hundred years permeating through rock, then marvel at the time and dedication the distillery puts into making its whisky. With its rugged coastline and bracing breezes, just being around Glenmorangie's distillery makes you feel healthy and vital, too. Though it means quite a long trek through the Scottish Highlands, the journey to this particular distillery is well worth the effort.

The distillery at Glenmorangie

Glen Moray

SPEYSIDE

Elgin, Speyside
www.glenmoray.com

Core range
Glen Moray Classic, 12- and 16-year-olds

Signature malt
Glen Moray 12-year-old: classic Speyside whisky with fruit, honey and malt all in balance - simple, but beautifully executed

Special occasions
The 1991 Mountain Oak Malt
The Final Release: spicy, warming and richly sweet, with a hint of ginger

For many years Glen Moray serviced the discount end of the market in its younger forms, and was excellent but little known at older ages. It was bought a few years ago by French company La Martiniquaise and since then it has been carefully repositioned without great fanfare. It's often overlooked, but shouldn't be as it has some delightful Speyside malts.

Glen Ord

HIGHLANDS

Muir of Ord, Ross-shire
www.discovering
distilleries.com

Signature malt
Glen Ord 12-year-old

Glen Ord is one of owner Diageo's biggest producing distilleries, but it is something of a journeyman malt, and a succession of name changes has done little to help it build a reputation.

Diageo is targeting the Asian markets, where The Macallan has long been dominant. To compete, Diageo needed a sherried whisky to rival Macallan's, so the sherry cask content in Glen Ord has been upped, and the whisky rebranded for Taiwan as The Singleton of Glen Ord. With malt in short supply, allocation of supplies to overseas territories has perhaps been inevitable. Let's hope the trickle of malts going down this route doesn't become a flood.

Glenrothes

SPEYSIDE

Rothes, Aberlour
www.glenrotheswhisky.com

Core range
The Glenrothes Select Reserve & Vintages

Signature malt
The Glenrothes Select Reserve: honey, fruit and spices from perfect oak casks – magnificent

Special occasions
Any Vintage of the 1970s: few distilleries put out such consistently fine malts

The distillery is a big producer, providing whiskies for several blends, including Cutty Sark. The single malt is the epitome of sophistication and style. It is packaged in distinctive, grenade-shaped bottles with hand-written labels. The vintages split two ways: citrussy with grapefruit, or sherried with red berries, the latter occasionally straying into earthy, almost sulphury territory. Mostly very good, though.

Glen Scotia

HIGHLANDS

Glen Scotia
www.lochlomonddistillery.com

Core range
Glen Scotia 12-year-old
Glen Scotia 17-year-old

Signature malt
Glen Scotia 12-year-old

Campbeltown on the west coast of Scotland used to be a rich and vibrant whisky-producing region. It saw no fewer than 34 distilleries set up here in its 19th-century heyday. Now just two are producing whisky for the market, Glen Scotia and Springbank, with Glengyle set to become the third. Now run by Loch Lomond Distillery Company, Glen Scotia produces only 750,000 litres a year, making it one of Scotland's smallest producers. Though a relatively rare malt, if you can track down an independent bottling, it will be something to treasure.

Glen Spey

SPEYSIDE

Rothes, Morayshire
www.malts.com

Signature malt
Glen Spey Flora & Fauna 12-year-old

There is considerable debate among Speyside lovers as to which town is the spiritual capital of the region. Certainly Rothes, rich in history and blessed with four working distilleries, has a strong case to argue.

The least known of the four Rothes distilleries, Glen Spey is one of those Diageo Speyside workhorses that make malt primarily for the blended whisky market – in this case, particularly for J&B. Although single malt bottlings are rare, there have been a number of independent releases and, a few years ago, a 12-year-old was released in Diageo's Flora and Fauna range.

Glentauchers

SPEYSIDE

Mulben, Keith, Banffshire

One of the anonymous but sizeable producing distilleries now owned by Pernod Ricard in Speyside, Glentauchers produces 3.4 million litres of spirit a year for inclusion in Ballantine's blended whisky. Pernod Ricard has ambitious plans for this internationally well-known blend, so Glentauchers' future would seem secure as one of its key malt suppliers. Single malt bottlings remain very rare, even though several whisky writers rave about the Glentauchers malt.

Glenturret

HIGHLANDS

Crieff, Perthshire
www.famousgrouse.co.uk

Signature malt
10-year-old: rich, bold and honeyed, with a strong malt backbone

Special occasions
The Whisky Exchange in London and Douglas Laing have both released 27-year-old independent bottlings

Glenturret has a fine pedigree. It was founded in 1775 and may well be the oldest working distillery in Scotland. It is small, producing about 300,000 litres per year, and most of the output goes into The Famous Grouse, which is the best-selling blend in Scotland. That doesn't leave much whisky for single malt bottlings, but there have been occasional releases in the past as well as, unusually, blended malts containing Glenturret and other single malt whiskies.

Highland Park

SLANDS

irkwall, Orkney
www.highlandpark.co.uk

ore range
ighland Park 12-, 15-, 16-, 18-, 25- and 30-year-olds

ignature malt
ighland Park 12-year-old: oft fruits wrapped in oney and rounded off vith a gentle smokiness

pecial occasions
he 18-year-old: the rademark honey, malt nd fruit are given an extra dimension by the presence of ood, smoke and spice

ighland Park lies on rugged and weather-swept rkney, and its malt is equally hardy. But Orkney is a varming, soulful place too, and the malt is outstanding, ombining fruit, honey, spice oak and a degree of eat from barley malted on site. HP has a large ollowing, with good reason.

Inchgower

SPEYSIDE

Buckie, Banffshire
www.malts.com

Signature malt
Inchgower Flora & Fauna 14-year-old: sweet and inoffensive Speyside malt, with a touch of earthiness, and even saltiness

Inchgower has the capacity to produce a sizeable amount of whisky – in excess of two million litres each year – though most of it is used for owner Diageo's heavyweight blends, including Bell's and Johnnie Walker. However, Diageo has released an Inchgower 22-year-old and 27-year-old as part of its Rare Malts series, both of which are excellent.

It's a pretty distillery, situated near the coast in the north of the Speyside region; the coastal proximity might explain why it's not a typically sweet Speysider

Jura

ISLANDS

Craighouse, Isle of Jura
www.isleofjura.com

Core range
Jura 10-year-old
Jura 16-year-old Superstition
Jura 21-year-old

Signature malt
Jura 10-year-old: young and fresh tasting with some melon in the malt and a trace of smoke

Special occasions
Jura 21-year-old Cask Strength

Though it often seems to be in the shadow of the whisky metropolis across the water on Islay, Jura is a top-notch distillery and produces a very fine malt in its own right. In recent years it has also proved that it can match its neighbour with a big peated whisky called Prophecy, and it also does a lightly peated whisky called Superstition. Jura is one of the world's best-selling single malts.

Kilchoman

ISLAY

Rockside Farm, Bruichladdich, Islay
www.kilchomandistillery.com

Core range
Kilchoman 5-year-old
Machir Bay range
Loch Gorm

Signature malt
Machir Bay: hitting top-notch balance now, with sweetness, fruit and peppery peat the perfect advert for the distillery and its location

How time flies! It seems like only yesterday that this small distillery opened on farmland, using local ingredients and producing precocious young and peaty spirit. It's growing up fast, though, and has earned its spurs as a genuine Islay player. It is yet to reach its best, but the malt takes another major step up every year and has started to branch out with unusual wood finishes. On the island of Islay there are two more distilleries on the horizon, so it's no longer the island's baby. A remarkable success story.

Kininvie

SPEYSIDE

Dufftown, Moray

Kininvie is one of Scottish whisky's best-kept secrets. It is hidden away behind Glenfiddich and Balvenie distilleries, and, although its owner William Grant has talked about releasing a single malt from Kininvie, this has yet to happen. The distillery's purpose is to provide malt for blending, such as for William Grant's Monkey Shoulder blended malt whisky, and, so far, it has been fully employed in this pursuit. Perhaps, now that the company has opened a new malt distillery to ensure supplies in the future, there will be sufficient whisky at Kininvie for it to be bottled in its own right.

Knockando

SPEYSIDE

Knockando, Aberlour, Banffshire
www.malts.com

Core range
Knockando 12-, 18- and 21-year-olds, plus other vintages without age statements

Although regarded as an elegant and complex whisky, Knockando has had only a very small presence in the single malt market in the UK. On the Continent and in the US, however, it is more widely distributed. Un-aged single malt bottlings do appear in the UK from time to time, and in some markets older expressions of Knockando are released. The malt is also one of the key whiskies in the J&B blend.

Knockdhu

HIGHLANDS

Knock, By Huntly,
Aberdeenshire

Core range
anCnoc 12-, 16- and
30-year-olds
anCnoc 1991

Signature malt
anCnoc 12-year-old:
a bit of everything here
- spice, malt, oak and
fruit, in perfect balance

Special occasions
anCnoc 30-year-old: not
for the faint-hearted, but
worth seeking out if you
like big, bold, oaky whisky

The distillery is called Knockdhu, but, because it was often confused with nearby Knockandu, owner Inver House decided to call the single malt by its Gaelic name, anCnoc ("the hill"). Its complex, earthy and clean taste owes much to traditional production methods.

Lagavulin

ISLAY

Port Ellen, Islay
www.malts.com

Core range
Lagavulin 12-year-old Cask Strength
Lagavulin 16-year-old
Distiller's Edition Double Matured

Signature malt
Lagavulin 16-year-old: a masterclass in peat working at different levels

Special occasions
Lagavulin 12-year-old: bottlings of this have been relatively common in recent years, and they vary from supercharged peaty dynamos to sweet and zesty peat-lite whiskies. They're always excellent.

Along with Ardbeg and Laphroaig, Lagavulin completes a "holy trinity" of distilleries in southeast Islay that have perfected the smoky and phenolic style of whisky for which the island is famous.

Like Ardbeg and Laphroaig, Lagavulin has the sea lapping at its doorstep and is everything you'd hope that a distillery should be. Lagavulin's warehouses are among the most atmospheric you'll find anywhere in Scotland.

In recent years, Lagavulin has suffered some major stock shortages, and its absence has made many hearts grow all the fonder. No-one has ever doubted its quality, but the shortages have given it what can only be described as an iconic status.

Lagavulin 16-year-old is a true giant from the peated isle. A massive dose of peat on the nose; equally strong and smoky on the palate, with cocoa and liquorice, and a rich, deep, growling body. Stunning!

Laphroaig

ISLAY

Port Ellen, Isle of Islay
www.laphroaig.com

Core range
Laphroaig 10-year-old
Laphroaig 10-year-old Cask Strength
Laphroaig 18-year-old
Laphroaig 25-year-old
Laphroaig 30-year-old
Laphroaig Quarter Cask

Signature malt
Laphroaig Quarter Cask: this offers new whisky enthusiasts an opportunity to experience the unique peat characteristics of Laphroaig without the full flavour bombardment that typifies the 10-year-old

Special occasions
If you find a bottle of 27-year-old and can afford it, just go for it. But otherwise the 18-year-old is delightful and a must for fans of peated whisky.

Laphroaig (pronounced "Laff-roy-g") is probably the most iconic Islay brand – the Marmite of whisky, which you either love or hate. Those who love it, tend to really, really love it; and for whom few other malts can compare.

First impressions of Laphroaig are that it's all smoke, fish and medicine. But spend some time with it, and there is an impressive array of flavours behind the Vesuvian-like sardine and smoke attack. As an entry level malt, ry the Quarter Cask. This is a vhisky finished in smaller casks, accelerating the maturation and softening the peat attack to great effect.

f you want to walk the tightrope vithout a safety net, then Scotch doesn't get much better than the o-year-old Cask Strength. This is massive peat attack, along with he richest malt and fruit double vhammy found in any malt.

few years back the atypical 15-year-old was eplaced with an 18-year-old expression that added ed liquorice to the peaty taste-fest and became an istant classic in the range.

Linkwood

SPEYSIDE

Elgin, Morayshire
www.malts.com

Signature malt
Linkwood 12-year-old: more floral than fruity; wispy, subtle and rounded

Linkwood is one of the most attractive and intriguing distilleries in Scotland. The whisky is highly respected; the distillery location, surrounded as it is with a nature reserve, is quite wonderful; and the strange production set-up keeps the "trainspotters" in business for hours.

There are two sets of stills on site: one set produces the bulk of the spirit, while an older set is employed for some of the year to produce a different spirit; the two are then mixed before filling to cask. Linkwood's distinctive whisky is particularly popular among blenders, while rare bottlings of single malt, whether official or through the independent sector, are much sought after by a hardcore band of devotees.

Loch Lomond

HIGHLANDS

Alexandria, Dumbartonshire
www.lochlomonddistillery.com

Loch Lomond is like no other distillery in Scotland, and has more in common with one of the large Irish or Canadian distilleries, with pot stills, a grain plant and "rectifiers" all employed to make a range of different whisky styles, most of which are used for the company's own blends. The reason for producing so many types is to help overcome shortages of malt, a problem that may well be reappearing for independent blenders as demand for whisky rises. So Loch Lomond, Old Rhosdhu (sometimes bottled as a surprisingly youthful 5-year-old) and Inchmurrin all hail from here.

The many styles of whisky mean that there is no recognisable style, and in fact single malts are relatively rare. But when they have appeared they have been of an impressively high standard.

Longmorn

SPEYSIDE

Elgin, Morayshire

Signature malt
Longmorn 16-year-old: a rich, complex and weighty malt; and, at 48% abv, a big hitter all round

Special occasions
Longmorn 17-year-old Distillers Edition: a masterpiece at cask strength – an oral pillow fight as fruit, oak and barley all battle for supremacy. Exceptional!

Longmorn is the whisky equivalent of a cult French-language film – adored by aficionados of the cinematic art; ignored in other quarters. Or, at least, that was the case. Owner Pernod Ricard seemed content to allow the whisky's reputation to rest on the back of some outstanding independent bottlings until a few years ago, when a cask strength 17-year-old was released. That has since been followed by an official 16-year-old release.

Macallan

SPEYSIDE

Craigellachie, Moray
www.themacallan.com

Core range
Fine Oak range
Sherry Oak range
Gold
Amber
Sienna
Ruby
1824 series

Signature malt
The Macallan Fine Oak 15-year-old: a mix of bourbon and sherry cask whisky that is laced with cocoa, orange and dried fruits, and lays bare the rich quality of The Macallan's malt

Special occasions
The Macallan Sherry Oak 18-year-old: quite possibly the perfect age for a Scotch single malt. The oak tempers the sherry here, while spices, dried lemon, orange peel and an underlying sweetness all combine to produce a classic single malt

Famed for its attention to detail, its refusal to cut corners and for the quality of its sherried whiskies,

The Macallan has long enjoyed a loyal and passionate following.

Macallan really became the complete package when it launched its Fine Oak range a few years ago. By combining sherry and bourbon casks, The Macallan has reined in the dominant winey notes and created a clean, fresh and sophisticated range of whiskies. The Fine Oak 15-year-old is the best expression of this range.

Most recently, owners Edrington withdrew some aged expressions from some markets, replacing them with four un-aged whiskies named by colour.

The distillery itself is beautiful, set high on an estate overlooking the Spey. At its centre is Easter Elchies House, now used to entertain guests. The still house is highly impressive, with small squat stills like beer-bellied penguins. The distillery is open to visitors most of the year.

Macduff

SPEYSIDE

Macduff, near Banff

Core range
Glen Deveron 10-and 15-year-olds

Signature malt
Glen Deveron 10-year-old

Confusingly, the small amount of single malt produced by Macduff Distillery is bottled under the name Glen Deveron, which alludes to the local river. The distillery was opened in the 1960s to provide blending stock, notably for William Lawson, but the malt is worthy of investigation in its own right because it is atypical of Speyside whiskies.

Mannochmore

SPEYSIDE

By Elgin, Morayshire
www.malts.com

Signature malt
Mannochmore 12-year-old

Lying to the south of Elgin, Mannochmore was established in 1971 to help provide malt for the Haig blend during a boom time for whisky. Consequently, Mannochmore is a rare beast as a single malt.

The distillery is famed for having produced the “black whisky” Loch Dhu, a decidedly average whisky that is, nevertheless, still in demand among collectors. An empty bottle once sold on eBay for £80, and when independent retailer The Whisky Shop released some Loch Dhu from its vaults, the bottles were selling for £175.

The malt, if you can find it, is a no-nonsense, relatively delicate but pleasant Speysider.

Miltonduff

SPEYSIDE

Elgin, Morayshire

Miltonduff is another of the great distilleries formerly owned by the Canadian whisky giant Hiram Walker. The distillery's purpose remains primarily to produce blending malts. It went through a period of using Lomond stills – which were designed to produce an array of different styles of malt from the same still. The experiment was abandoned because Lomond stills are inefficient and notoriously difficult to clean, but, while they operated, the whisky produced was known as Mosstowie, bottles of still appear from time to time. These days, Miltonduff has the capacity to produce more than five million litres of malt, and it is a key component of Ballantine's. The distillery was acquired in 2005 by Pernod Ricard, which has since made Miltonduff its trade and production headquarters.

Mortlach

SPEYSIDE

Dufftown, Banffshire
www.malts.com

Signature malt
Mortlach 16-year-old: a flavour-rich, chunky, oily and quirky malt, which tastes like nothing else on Speyside

Whisky enthusiasts adore Mortlach. It has a complex and unique distillation process that includes a motley crew of stills and a partial triple distillation, which ensures that all sorts of compounds are kept in the mix to give the whisky a variety of subtle nuances unlike anything else in the region.

Blenders love Mortlach too, and it is widely considered to be an "adhesive malt" that can bring lots of other flavours to order. The distillery is sizeable, and capable of producing three million litres of spirit a year.

A very small amount of 32-year-old Mortlach was released a few years ago.

Oban

HIGHLANDS

Oban, Argyll
www.malts.com

Core range
Oban 14-year-old
Oban 1980 Distillers Edition
Double Matured
Oban 32-year-old

Signature malt
Oban 14-year-old: a growling, purring vehicle that moves up the gears from gentle start to rich, fruity and reasonably smoky monster; full and intriguing

Oban's distillery is in the heart of the pretty sea port. It drips with character and charm, and still uses worm tubs to cool the spirit from the stills, making for a characterful final whisky. The coastal location and the distinctive peatiness of the malt makes it one of the finest Highland distilleries to visit.

Old Pulteney

HIGHLANDS

Wick, Caithness
www.oldpulteney.com

Core range
Old Pulteney 12-, 17- and 21-year-olds

Signature malt
Old Pulteney 12-year-old: outstanding tangy, salty seaside character and plenty of Highland bite; a rich whisky and a very moreish one

Special occasions
The 17-year-old: citrus fruits, rich malt and the trademark salt with some spice make this very hard to resist; for a treat, this is not too pricey either

Based in the far north of Scotland at Wick, it's a long way to go for a visit, but this charming and quirky distillery is worth it. The malts vary considerably over the range, but the saltiness and citrus of the 12-year-old is irresistible and moreish.

Port Charlotte

ISLAY

Bruichladdich,
Isle of Islay
www.bruichladdich.com

Port Charlotte has an almost legendary status among whisky fans, having once been the name of a distillery on Islay. The heavily peated and distinctive style was recreated by Bruichladdich a few years back, sending fans in to raptures. The old site is being redeveloped on the shore of Loch Indaal and with another new distillery enterprise across the Loch, the race is on to see which will make it as Islay's ninth distillery. Certainly these are heady days for Scotland's whisky isle.

Roseisle

HIGHLANDS

Elgin, Northern Highlands
www.diageo.com

We're going to have to wait some time yet to taste Roseisle single malt; it won't be bottled for a few years until it's 12 years old. Quite what it will taste like is anyone's guess because the distillery is purpose-built to create two very different malts to fill gaps in Diageo's overall taste spectrum, which it uses for making its blends.

It looks more like a factory, and it is Scotland's biggest malt whisky producer, having started production in 2009 to produce up to 12 million litres of malt in two separate styles, mainly to help the company grow its blended portfolio in emerging markets over the next few years. It's a state-of-the-art plant, environmentally friendly, and with a number of innovative features to make the workforce's work as un-labour-intensive as possible. A single malt will eventually be bottled, but the priority is most certainly blended whisky.

Royal Brackla

SPEYSIDE

Cawdor, Nairn

Signature malt
Royal Brackla 10-year-old:
a rich and rewarding sweet Speyside

Royal Brackla is situated in Cawdor, home of the castle that features in Shakespeare's *Macbeth*. In 2012 it celebrated its 200th anniversary, having opened in 1812, and is one of only three distilleries to have been allowed to use the prefix "Royal" – an honour granted because William IV was partial to this whisky. Most of the production goes for blending.

Royal Lochnagar

HIGHLANDS

Balmoral
www.malts.com

Signature malt
Royal Lochnagar 12-year-old

Special occasions
Selected Reserve Royal Lochnagar: a limited edition release, often aged for about 20 years

Royal Lochnagar is Diageo's smallest distillery and one of its prettiest, nestling on the edge of the Balmoral estate, the Scottish home of the Royal Family. It is entitled to use the prefix "royal" because Queen Victoria visited the distillery in 1848 and took a liking to it. It maintains old-fashioned equipment such as wooden washbacks and "worms" – flat-lying copper pipes for condensing spirit that pass through a pool of cool water on the distillery roof. Two small stills and a long fermentation period contribute to a distinctive and weighty whisky.

Scapa

ISLANDS

St Ola, Kirkwall, Orkney
www.scapamalt.com

Signature malt
Scapa 14-year-old: zesty, fresh and moreish, with ripe melon, lemon and honey flavours

Until a few years ago, Scapa was an extremely rare whisky. The distillery was all but abandoned, producing spirit for only a few weeks a year to top up supplies. However, it was refurbished and put back into production in 2003. Pernod Ricard then took it over from Allied Domecq. As a result of the changes, the standard 14-year-old is now more readily available and worth seeking out.

Try some of Scapa's older and cask strength expressions, which have a barley intensity and some salt and peat notes that generate a rewarding level of complexity.

Speyburn

SPEYSIDE

Rothes, Speyside
www.inverhouse.com

Signature malt
Speyburn 10-year-old:
clean and simple, sweet and
with the faintest smoke undertow

Special occasions
Speyburn 25-year-old Solera Cask:
not an easy whisky to pin down
because its style is evolving.
But what you can expect is the age
showing through, with the Speyburn
sweetness tempered by spice and oak
from the wood

Speyburn lies in the heart of Speyside. The district is verdant and beautiful, and Speyburn's pagoda-style chimneys make it an archetypal Speysider. However, much of Speyburn's malt is exported to America, and it is not particularly known in its own right in Europe.

Speyside

SPEYSIDE

Drumguish
www.speysidedistillery.co.uk

Core range
Drumguish
Speyside 8-, 10- and 12-year-olds

Signature malt
Speyside 12-year-old: the richest and fullest of the distillery's malts

This is a neat and compact distillery, a long way to the south of the area most associated with Speyside but, nevertheless, close to a major tributary of the Spey River. The distillery was used in the filming of the *Monarch of the Glen* TV series, but, in terms of whisky making, it is something of a secret to many.

Speyside produces a range of malts, and the company has its own Glasgow-based operation for blending and bottling its whisky. It is not a big player in the UK, and it's fair to assume that a great deal of the distillery's whisky goes abroad.

Springbank

HIGHLANDS

Campbeltown, Argyll
www.springbankdistillers.com

Core range
Springbank 10-year-old,
15-year-old and 25-year-old
Springbank 10-year-old 100 Proof

Signature malt
Springbank 10-year-old, 100 Proof:
a full malt like no other – blatant
and colourful, yet nuanced,
unpredictable and engaging

Springbank is a "three whiskies" distillery. In addition to the eponymous malt, it also produces Longrow, a significantly peated whisky, and Hazelburn, which is triple distilled. And, since 2004, it has also had a sibling called Glengyle – the first new distillery in Campbeltown for 125 years; it produces a malt called Kilkerran. The distillery is rustic, artisanal and traditional, and although Campbeltown is hard to reach, devotees flock to it. Springbank whisky itself is robust, challenging and very well made.

Strathisla

SPEYSIDE

Keith, Banffshire
www.chivas.com

Core range
Strathisla 12-year-old
Strathisla 18-year-old

Signature malt
Strathisla 12-year-old: rich, sherried and satisfying, with a nice platform of sweet fruits

Special occasions
Strathisla 15-year-old Cask Strength: bolder, oakier and arguably drier than the standard bottling; the extra strength gives it added depth

Strathisla is the oldest working distillery in the Highlands, and its maturation warehouse contains some of Chivas Brothers' oldest stock, along with rare and special casks, including one that is owned by Prince Charles. Strathisla is a fine whisky and it plays a key role in the outstanding Chivas blend.

Strathmill

SPEYSIDE

Keith, Banffshire
www.malts.com

Signature malt
Strathmill 12-year-old: Released as part of the Flora and Fauna series, Strathmill is sweet, honeyed and floral, with a hint of orange

Strathmill is one of those classic and traditional distilleries that ticks all the boxes when it comes to the romance of malt. It is a pretty distillery, with twin pagoda chimneys, situated by the side of a river in the town of Keith, the epicentre of Speyside.

Production capacity is sizeable and the process includes a purifier that's designed to create a light style of whisky, much in demand for blending – particularly for J&B. A 12-year-old single malt was released for the first time in 2001, as part of Diageo's Flora and Fauna range.

Talisker

ISLANDS

Carbost, Isle of Skye

Core range
Talisker 10-year-old
1986 Distillers Edition Double Matured
Talisker 18-year-old
Talisker 25-year-old
Talisker 57 Degrees North

Signature malt
Talisker 10-year-old: classic pepper and smoke explosion; a dry storm of a whisky

Special occasions
Talisker 18-year-old: this has everything – lots of smoke, the trademark pepper and spice, a honeycomb heart and a three-dimensional, chunky depth not present in the 10-year-old. It is whisky at its most wonderful

Nestling among the rocky crags and rugged shoreline of Skye, Talisker is in perfect harmony with its desolate surroundings. So too is its whisky, which reflects the wild, stark landscape. Skye is a rugged and unforgiving island, which has witnessed some of the country's bloodiest and most dramatic history. Traditionally, its climate has been harsh and challenging. Unsurprisingly, then, there's an earthiness about the people and the place. But there's an other-worldliness to Skye, too, as if you have been transported to another planet. Both the distillery and the whisky echo this environment, and Talisker is a bold and confident malt – and decidedly masculine.

Talisker 18-year-old was voted the best malt in the world in the first World Whisky Awards, organised by *Whisky Magazine* in 2007, and with good reason. The trademark Talisker pepper and fire remains in place, but the age gives it a sweeter third dimension – faultless.

Tamdhu

SPEYSIDE

Knockando, Aberlour

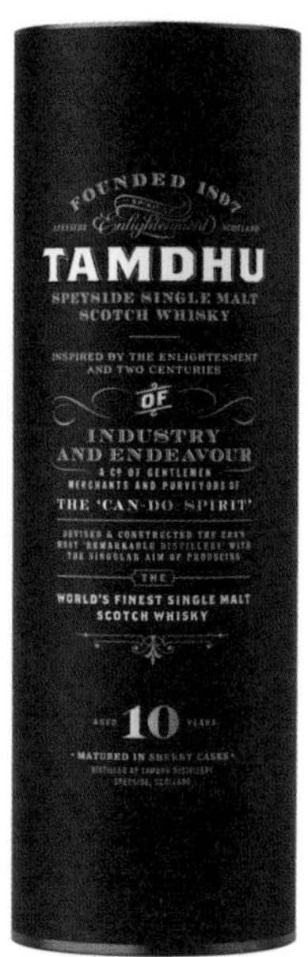

Tamdhu lost its way some years ago, its place in the Edrington portfolio a lowly one. But it is now in the hands of the independent whisky company Ian Macleod, who also own Glengoyne. The old "Saladin box" method of malting is no longer being used, but this unique piece of equipment, along with the distillery's own railway station and impressive buildings, will make this a great distillery to tour when the new owners have smartened it up. The first new whiskies emerged in the summer of 2013, two different styles of 10-year-old malt. But malt aficionados are looking forward to special and older zesty and sherbetty releases from the distillery's sizeable stocks. Independent bottlings have often been superb.

Tamnavulin

SPEYSIDE

Ballindalloch, Banffshire

Core range
Tamnavulin 12-year-old

When Indian businessman Vijay Mallya held a press conference to announce his purchase of Whyte & Mackay, he pulled the rabbit out of the hat by announcing the reopening of Tamnavulin Distillery after 12 non-productive years. In 2007 the output was a modest one million litres but in 2008 the distillery reached full production of about four million litres, doubling Whyte & Mackay's output.

Tamnavulin was built in 1966 – a newish distillery – and is functional rather than pretty, though it does lie in the scenic heart of the Livet Valley, on a tributary to the River Livet. Little of the previous production was ever bottled as a single malt.

Teaninich

HIGHLANDS

Alness, Ross-Shire
www.malts.com

Signature malt
Teaninich 10-year-old

Global drinks corporation Diageo has a number of Speyside distilleries that operate in the shadows, and none more so than Teaninich. Close to the relatively famous Dalmore, Teaninich is a sizeable distillery capable of producing more than 2.5 million litres per annum, yet it is virtually unknown in its own right.

The whisky has a couple of quirky production characteristics that are of interest to the technically-minded, but, for the most part, Teaninich slips under the radar. A bottling did appear in Diageo's Flora and Fauna range some years back, but otherwise, as a single malt, Teaninich is very much a rarity.

Tobermory

ISLANDS

Tobermory, Isle of Mull
www.burnstewartdistillers.com

Core range
Tobermory 10- and 15-year-olds, Ledaig 10-year-old

Signature malt
Tobermory 10-year-old: light and refreshing, with a blemish-free hit of malt through its heart

Tobermory was something of a lightweight whisky until a few years back, though it did perk up when enriched with age in good-quality sherry casks. But the owners upped the strength of the malt and no longer chill-filter it, which leaves in fat and flavour compounds. This has made for a much better, more robust and deliciously sweet island whisky. The distillery also produced peated whisky under the name Ledaig.

Tomatin

HIGHLANDS

Tomatin, Inverness-shire
www.tomatin.com

Signature malt
Tomatin 12-year-old: a balanced and easy-going, yet full Highland whisky

In 1974, Tomatin was the biggest producer in Scotland. It still has the capacity to produce a significant five million litres of spirit each year, yet Tomatin is a strange beast, and not as well known as perhaps it might be. The main reason for this is because most of its whisky goes abroad, either as single malt or through a number of blends, most notably The Antiquary. Occasionally, the distillery bottles vintage expressions, which are worth seeking out. In the past few years, there have been bottlings from 1973 and 1965.

In 1986, Tomatin became the first Scottish distillery to come under Japanese ownership.

Tomintoul

SPEYSIDE

Ballindalloch, Banffshire
www.tomintouldistillery.com

Core range
Tomintoul 10-, 16- and 27-year-olds

Signature malt
Tomintoul 16-year-old: arguably the best value-for-money single malt in Speyside, commanding a modest price, but rich in fruit, malt and oak – stunning

Tomintoul can produce more than three million litres of spirit each year, and, since the turn of the millennium, it has been owned by independent bottler Angus Dundee. In that time, Tomintoul has been quietly building up its reputation as a single malt, and the 16-year-old is particularly impressive. The distillery has also launched a peated whisky called Old Ballantruan, and, along with BenRiach, is seriously challenging some preconceptions about the region.

Tormore

SPEYSIDE

Advie by Grantown-on-Spey,
Morayshire
www.tormore.com

Signature malt
Tormore 12-year-old: easy-drinking, clean and soft

Designed to be a showcase distillery, Tormore is among Scotland's quirkiest distilleries, with oddball features such as a musical clock. In recent years it has become another sizeable producer of malts intended for blends such as Ballantine's and Teacher's. Pernod Ricard now owns the distillery and has launched a delightful 12-year-old single malt, suggesting that the distillery might be set for a spot in the limelight.

Tullibardine

HIGHLANDS

Blackford, Perthshire
www.tullibardine.com

Signature malt
Tullibardine 10-year-old

Tullibardine had been mothballed for nine years when a consortium came together to buy the facility and its stocks in 2003. The first releases since then have come from the archives and include some whiskies that are more than 30 years old. The marketing of the whisky shows a modern approach, coupled with a strong emphasis on heritage (the shop and café are called 1488, to highlight the fact that beer was brewed on the site more than 500 years ago). The distillery's owners have not been afraid to try new ideas, and the policy seems to have paid off. But, as an independent, Tullibardine has been vulnerable to the threat of a takeover, and, in late 2008, the company was said to be considering its options for the future.

Index

Acknowledgements

The publishers would like to thank the following for their assistance with images:

Bacardi, Balmenach Distillery, BenRiach Distillery, Berry Brothers & Rudd Ltd, The Big Partnership, Bruichladdich Distillery, Burn Stewart Distillers Ltd, Chivas Brothers, CL WorldBrands Ltd, Cognis PR, Diego, The Edrington Group, Fortune Brands Inc, Glenmorangie, Highland Park, Highland Distillers Plc, Inver House Distillers, Isle of Arran Distillers, John Dewar and Sons Ltd, Margaret PR, Morrison Bowmore Distillers Ltd, Pernod Ricard, Richmond Towers, Tobermory Distillery, Touch PR, Whyte and Mackay Ltd, William Grant and Sons.

Cover image: Diageo Claive Vidiz collection, the largest Scotch Whisky collection in the world on July 10, 2012 in Edinburgh, Scotland, UK.